FADE IN

The Essential Skills for Acting

Debanshu Shekhar

15 Methods to Master the 'BASICS of ACTING' for Stage and Screen

<u>Preface</u>

Welcome to "**FADE IN**"- A book that dives into the world of acting and storytelling. In this book, we'll explore what it means to be an actor and how to bring characters to life, on stage or screen.

As an actor myself, I have first-hand experience of the transformative power of storytelling. Each role undertaken is a chance to inhabit another world, to explore the depths of human emotion and to connect with audiences at a profound level.

Through this book I wanted to share with you all what I've discovered in my 12 years journey as a theatre actor. **"FADE IN"** has stemmed out of the passion that I have for this art form and a desire to share my insights, techniques and the lessons learned along the way.

This book can be your comprehensive guide to hone your craft by understanding an actor's instrument to mastering stage presence; from building authentic connections with fellow actors to entering the audition room with confidence.

Whether you're a seasoned performer or just starting your journey, **"FADE IN"** has something for everyone, providing practical advice, thought-provoking exercises, and inspiration to fuel your artistic growth.

I hope this book helps you in your journey as an actor.

Remember to enjoy the process, learn from your experiences and always strive to be true to yourself on stage or in front of the camera.

Best wishes,

Debanshu Shekhar.

Acknowledgement

I would like to express my heartfelt gratitude to each and every individual who has contributed to the creation of this book.

First and foremost, I extend my deepest appreciation to my brother Amritanshu Shekhar, for his unwavering support that motivated me to write this book.

I'm grateful to all the teachers at my Drama School, Bhartendu Natya Academy (B.N.A) Lucknow, and all the mentors, coaches and directors who have shared their wisdom and guidance with me over the years. Your invaluable insights have shaped my understanding of acting and storytelling.

To my friends from Delhi University, my fellow actors, my seniors & juniors from B.N.A, Rangshila Theatre Group Mumbai, and NSPA (Natural Streets for Performing Arts) thank you for sharing your experiences and insights with me.

Last but not least, I want to thank my wife Srishti Sharma, for always supporting me. Your enthusiasm and encouragement inspire me to continue pursuing my passion for acting, direction and writing.

Thankful for everyone and all the experiences…

Love and light!

Debanshu Shekhar.

Introduction

Welcome to **"FADE IN"**. This book is for all the people who are actors at heart- whether you are planning to pursue acting as a full-time profession or you're just enthusiastic about it or you've been acting for a while, there's something here for each one of you.

In **"FADE IN"**, you'll find techniques, exercises and key insights to help you hone your craft. This book will definitely be a step in grooming yourself into a better actor.

Acting isn't just about learning up a few dialogues and saying it out loud; it's about becoming someone else, adapting to different characters, making them believable, connecting with audiences and telling powerful stories. Through this book, we'll explore the various aspects of acting, from vocal and physical exercises to character development and audition techniques.

But acting isn't just about technique; it's also about passion, dedication, and a willingness to explore the depths of human emotion. As you journey through these pages, I encourage you to approach each exercise with an open mind and a sense of curiosity. Allow yourself to be vulnerable, to take risks, and to embrace the journey of self-discovery that acting offers.

Whether you dream of being on stage or in movies, or simply honing your acting skills for personal fulfillment, **"FADE IN"** is here to help you on your journey.

So, without further ado, let's dive in and discover the magic of acting together. The stage is set, the cameras are rolling – let the lights **FADE IN!**

All the Best.

<u>Outline</u>

PART 1: THE FOUNDATIONS OF ACTING

- **Chapter 1: Finding Your Voice:** Exploring vocal techniques for clarity, projection, and emotional expression.

- **Chapter 2: Unlocking Your Body:** Understanding body language, movement principles, and physical presence on stage and screen.

- **Chapter 3: Building Your Toolkit:** Delving into different acting methods (Stanislavski, Meisner, etc.) and their core principles.

- **Chapter 4: The Power of Observation:** Sharpening your observational skills to create authentic characters and believable emotions.

- **Chapter 5: Imagination: Your Fuel for Creation:** Unleashing your imagination to fuel character development, scene analysis, and improvisation.

PART 2: BUILDING YOUR CHARACTER

- **Chapter 6: Deciphering Emotions:** Exploring the spectrum of human emotions and expressing them truthfully through your craft.

- **Chapter 7: Bringing Words to Life:** Mastering diction, articulation, and textual analysis for impactful delivery.

- **Chapter 8: Embodying the Character:** Using costume, makeup, and physicality to enhance character portrayal and connect with the audience.

- **Chapter 9: Developing Your Instrument:** Practicing vocal and physical exercises to improve your overall acting ability.

PART 3: MASTERING THE CRAFT

- **Chapter 10: Focus and Concentration:** Maintaining focus in demanding situations and developing laser-sharp concentration for powerful performances.

- **Chapter 11: Creating Connection:** Building genuine relationships with fellow actors and understanding stage dynamics.

- **Chapter 12: Living in the Moment:** Cultivating spontaneity and reacting authentically to scene developments.

- **Chapter 13: Projecting Your Energy:** Commanding the stage or screen with confident projection and stage presence.

- **Chapter 14: Internalization and Truth:** Exploring techniques to connect emotionally with your character and find their inner truth.

- **Chapter 15: Conquering the Audition:** Mastering audition techniques, overcoming nerves, and showcasing your best self.

CHAPTER 1: Finding Your Voice
Unleashing the Power of Expression

Theory:

Your voice is your instrument as an actor. It's not just about volume and clarity, but the ability to express a vast range of emotions, thoughts, and intentions. A powerful voice can captivate audiences, draw them into the character's world, and evoke empathy. So, how do you find your voice and develop it into a versatile tool for storytelling?

Understanding Your Voice:
Your voice has various components:

- ***Pitch:*** The highness or lowness of your voice.
- ***Pace:*** Speed of your speech.
- ***Volume:*** Loudness or softness of your voice.
- ***Articulation:*** Clarity of pronunciation.
- ***Resonance:*** The richness and depth of sound.
- ***Intonation:*** Changes in pitch and tone to convey meaning.

Understanding the Power of Your Voice:

Your voice is more than just your speaking tool; it's an extension of your being. Through vocal expression, you breathe life into characters, captivate audiences, and paint emotional landscapes with sound. Mastering your voice unlocks its expressive potential, allowing you to deliver powerful performances that resonate long after the curtain falls.

Challenges to Vocal Expression:

- ***Nerves and Tension:*** Stage fright and anxiety can tighten your vocal cords, impacting vocal clarity and projection.
- ***Poor Posture and Breath Control:*** Slouching and shallow breathing impede vocal power and limit expressiveness.
- ***Limited Vocal Range and Dynamics:*** Monotonous delivery lacks impact and fails to convey the full spectrum of character emotions.
- ***Inattention to Diction and Articulation:*** Mumbling and unclear pronunciation hinder audience understanding and emotional connection.

Building Your Vocal Foundation:

- ***Warm-up:*** Dedicate time daily to vocal warm-up exercises. Humming, lip trills, and scales improve flexibility, range, and vocal clarity.
- ***Posture and Alignment:*** Stand tall, engage your core, and maintain proper neck and head alignment for optimal breath support and vocal projection.
- ***Breath Control:*** Practice diaphragmatic breathing exercises to ensure sustained vocal delivery and prevent vocal fatigue.
- ***Articulation and Diction:*** Enunciate clearly, emphasize consonants, and pronounce vowels accurately for optimal clarity and intelligibility.

Exercises for Vocal Empowerment:

- ***Tongue Twisters:*** Practice tongue twisters like "Peter Piper picked pickled peppers" to improve agility and articulation.
- ***Mirror Work:*** Deliver monologues while observing your posture, breath control, and facial expressions. Adjust them for optimal vocal impact.
- ***Vocal Improvisation:*** Explore creating sounds and expressing emotions solely through vocalization, pushing your comfort zone and expanding your range.
- ***Echo Reading:*** Practice echoing the pronunciation of another person, refining your ear for clarity and articulation.

Exploring Vocal Expression:

- ***Vocal Dynamics:*** Vary your volume, pitch, and pace to portray different emotions and emphasize key lines. Use silence purposefully to add depth and meaning.
- ***Emotional Exploration:*** Choose a scene with strong emotional content. Practice delivering lines while focusing on embodying the character's specific emotions through your voice.
- ***Character Voices:*** Explore different vocal qualities for different characters – age, personality, social background. Experiment with accents and dialects responsibly.
- ***Storytelling with Voice:*** Practice reading a story aloud, using vocal variety to depict different characters and build dramatic tension.

Beyond the Basics:

- ***Record Yourself:*** Record yourself performing scenes and monologues. Listen back critically and identify areas for improvement.
- ***Seek Feedback:*** Work with a vocal coach or acting teacher who can provide personalized feedback and tailored exercises.
- ***Observe and Learn:*** Watch skilled actors and analyze their vocal choices. Observe how they use their voice to convey emotions, connect with the audience, and tell the story.

Remember: Developing your voice is a journey, not a destination. Embrace the continuous learning process, experiment with different techniques, and never stop seeking ways to refine your vocal instrument. With dedication and practice, you'll find your unique voice, captivating audiences and bringing characters to life through the power of vocal expression.

Bonus Tip: Explore vocal warm-up apps and online resources to enrich your daily practice routine and discover diverse vocal exercises.

---------- **End of Chapter 1** ----------

CHAPTER 2: Unlocking Your Body
The Physical Language of Acting

Theory:

Your body is your canvas as an actor. It speaks volumes even before you utter a word. Every movement, posture, and gesture communicate emotions, intentions, and character traits. Mastering your body language not only enhances your stage presence but also deepens your connection with the character and the audience.

Understanding Body Language:
Body language comprises various elements-
- *Posture:* How you stand, sit, or hold yourself reflects confidence, nervousness, authority, or submission.
- *Gestures:* Hand and arm movements add emphasis, convey emotions, and reveal character traits.

- *Facial expressions:* The micro-movements of your face communicate a vast range of emotions and reactions.
- *Physical contact:* How you touch yourself or others (if the scene allows) reveals intimacy, power dynamics, or discomfort.
- *Eye contact:* Holding someone's gaze establishes connection, conveys sincerity, or reflects avoidance.

Challenges to Physical Expression:

- *Stage Fright and Tension:* Anxiety can manifest in stiff posture, limited movement, and hindered emotional expression through the body.
- *Lack of Awareness:* Unconscious habits, poor posture, and awkward gestures can distract from your character and weaken your stage presence.
- *Limited Movement Range:* Restricted movement and a static stage presence can limit your ability to fully inhabit your character and engage the audience.
- *Disconnecting Body and Voice:* Dissonance between vocal expression and physicality can create confusion and weaken the emotional impact of your performance.

Building Your Physical Foundation:

- *Body Awareness:* Practice mindfulness exercises and body scans to become acutely aware of your posture, tension, and physical habits.

- ***Alignment and Core Strength:*** Engage your core, maintain proper posture, and practice alignment exercises to create a strong foundation for expressive movement.
- ***Stretching and Flexibility:*** Regular stretching improves your range of motion, allowing for more fluid and nuanced physical expression.
- ***Neutral Movement:*** Master neutral movement principles (walking, standing, sitting) to create a foundation for building expressive character-specific movements.

Exercises to Unlock Your Body:

1. Body Awareness:

- Stand in front of a mirror and observe your posture, breathing, and natural stance.
- Notice any tension or imbalances. Engage in gentle stretches and relaxation techniques to improve body awareness.
- Practice different postures associated with specific emotions (confidence, fear, sadness) and observe how they feel physically.

2. Mirroring and Observation:

- Observe people around you – their posture, walk, gestures, and facial expressions in different situations.
- Practice mirroring their movements subtly to understand the communication behind them.

- Apply these observations to create believable physicality for your characters.

3. Improvisation and Movement Games:

- Participate in improvisation exercises that focus on physical responses to situations and stimuli.
- Play movement games like "statue" or "charades" to explore different emotional expressions through the body.
- Practice walking, running, and sitting with various emotions and intentions to embody diverse characters.

4. Yoga and Mindfulness:

- Yoga practices improve flexibility, coordination, and breath control, enhancing your physical expression.
- Mindfulness exercises cultivate body awareness and reduce tension, allowing you to move with authenticity.

5. Character Embodiment:

- Analyze your character's physical description, background, and personality.
- Imagine how they would stand, walk, and react in different situations.
- Practice embodying these physical traits while rehearsing lines and scenes.

Beyond the Basics:

- ***Physical Improvisation:*** Hone your improvisational skills by incorporating physical elements into improvised scenes and exercises. Embrace spontaneity in movement and gesture, allowing your body to respond instinctively to the given circumstances and your scene partners.
- ***Cross-Disciplinary Exploration:*** Draw inspiration from other movement-based disciplines such as dance, martial arts, or Kalaripayattu. Explore how principles from these disciplines can inform and enhance your approach to physicality and movement in acting.
- ***Character Physicality***: Move beyond generic movement patterns to develop distinct physicality for each character you portray. Experiment with different gestures, mannerisms, and physical quirks that reflect the character's personality, background, and motivations.

Remember: Unlocking your body is a continuous process. Explore different movement styles, study body language cues, and observe skilled actors to expand your physical vocabulary. Be authentic, avoid clichés, and allow your body to become a natural extension of your character.

Bonus Tip: Watch dance performances from various cultures and analyze how movement conveys emotions and stories. How can you incorporate these ideas into your own acting?

---------- End of Chapter 2 ----------

CHAPTER 3: Building Your Toolkit
Exploring Essential Acting Methods

Theory:

Stepping onto the stage or in front of the camera requires more than just memorizing lines. Every actor needs a toolkit filled with various approaches to breathe life into characters and connect with audiences. This chapter delves into three fundamental methods that lay the foundation for your acting journey:

1. Stanislavski's System:

Considered the "grandfather of modern acting," this method, developed by Konstantin Stanislavski, emphasizes building genuine emotions and understanding your character's inner life. Its core principles include:

- ***Emotional Memory:*** Drawing on personal experiences and emotions to connect with the character authentically. Imagine yourself in similar situations your character faces, tapping into genuine feelings.
- ***Units and Objectives:*** Breaking down scenes into smaller "units" and identifying your character's specific "objective" in each moment. What does your character want, and how are they trying to achieve it in each scene?

- ***Given Circumstances:*** Immersing yourself in the character's world, considering their background, relationships, and the overall situation of the play or film. This creates a foundation for believable behaviour and reactions.

Exercises:

- ***Monologue Exploration:*** Choose a monologue that resonates with you emotionally. Analyze the character's motivations and objectives in each moment. Try performing it while recalling a personal experience that evokes similar emotions.
- ***Sensory Immersion:*** Pick a scene from a play or film. Imagine yourself in the character's shoes. What do you see, hear, smell, and feel in that environment? Let these sensory details inform your physicality and emotions.
- ***Mirror Work:*** Practice mirroring expressions and gestures of people around you. Observe how their nonverbal communication conveys emotions and intentions. Adapt these observations to create believable physicality for your characters.

2. Meisner Technique:

Developed by Sanford Meisner, this method prioritizes living truthfully in the moment and reacting authentically to your fellow actors. Key principles include:

- ***Living in the Moment:*** Focusing solely on your scene partner and responding intuitively to their words and actions. Avoid planning reactions beforehand and allow genuine emotions to emerge in the moment.

- ***No Preconceived Ideas:*** Setting aside personal interpretations and responding naturally to what unfolds in the scene. This fosters spontaneity and keeps your performance fresh and engaging.
- ***Repetition and Emotional Growth:*** Repeatedly rehearsing scenes allows you to delve deeper, access genuine emotions, and build trust with your scene partner. The more you explore, the richer your performance becomes.

Exercises:

- ***Improv Games:*** Engage in improvisation exercises that focus on reacting instinctively to prompts and situations. This hones your ability to think on your feet and respond authentically.
- ***Scene Partner Work:*** Find a partner and practice scenes with the sole focus on responding truthfully to their actions and emotions. Let the scene unfold organically without planning your reactions.
- ***Emotional Recall:*** Choose a strong emotional memory from your life. Practice recalling it vividly while performing a monologue or scene. Observe how accessing genuine emotions impacts your delivery and presence.

3. Practical Aesthetics:

Developed by David Mamet, this method emphasizes clear communication and truthful storytelling through action and reaction. Its core principles include:

- ***The Given Circumstances:*** Analyzing the script to understand the character's physical and emotional situation. What are their specific circumstances, relationships, and goals?
- ***Action and Reaction:*** Defining your character's actions based on their wants and needs, and reacting instinctively to the actions of others. This creates a clear cause-and-effect dynamic in your performance.
- ***Truthful Communication:*** Delivering lines organically, avoiding artificiality, and focusing on clear meaning. Your voice and body should support the text's intent, ensuring the audience understands your message.

Exercises:

- ***Script Breakdown:*** Choose a scene from a play or film and analyze it thoroughly. Identify the character's objectives, "the given circumstances," and potential actions in each moment.
- ***Action-Reaction Studies:*** Watch scenes from films known for their realistic portrayals. Observe how characters react to each other's actions and how these reactions drive the story forward.
- ***Monologue Analysis:*** Select a monologue and examine its subtext and hidden messages. Practice delivering it with clear intention and focus on conveying the unspoken emotions behind the words.

Beyond the Basics:

- *Advanced Scene Analysis:* Dive deeper into scene analysis by exploring additional layers of subtext, theme, and character dynamics. Consider how cultural, historical, and contextual factors influence character motivations and relationships within the scene.
- *Script Adaptation and Interpretation:* Explore techniques for adapting and interpreting scripts from different genres, styles, and time periods. Experiment with how changes in language, pacing, and delivery can alter the audience's perception and emotional response to the material.
- *Method Acting Technique:* Explore advanced techniques within the Method acting approach, such as affective memory, emotional recall, and sense memory. Deepen your connection to the character's emotional truth by drawing on personal experiences and sensory details to inform your performance.

Remember: This is just the beginning of your exploration. These are not the only methods to hone your acting skills. Each method offers valuable tools, but the key is to find what resonates with you and create your own unique approach. Experiment, practice, and most importantly, embrace the journey of discovery!

Bonus Tip: Watch interviews with actors discussing their methods and approach to acting. Analyze their insights and connect them to the principles discussed in this chapter.

---------- **End of Chapter 3** ---------

CHAPTER 4: The Power of Observation
Fueling Your Acting Journey

Theory:

Great actors don't just memorize lines; they observe the world around them, collecting a treasure trove of details that breathe life into their characters. From subtle nuances in body language to the complexities of human emotions, the power of observation fuels authenticity and ignites captivating performances.

Why Observation Matters:

- ***Understanding Human Behaviour:*** By observing people in different situations, you learn how they express emotions, react to events, and interact with each other. This knowledge informs your character choices and creates believable portrayals.
- ***Building Character Details:*** Every character is unique, shaped by their background, personality, and experiences. Keen observation helps you gather specific details – mannerisms, speech patterns, even physical quirks – that enrich your characterization.

- ***Evoking Genuine Emotions:*** Observing real people and their emotional expressions allows you to tap into genuine emotions for your own performances. This makes your portrayals more relatable and impactful.
- ***Sparking Imagination:*** Observation fuels your creative engine. Observing diverse faces, gestures, and situations ignites your imagination and inspires unique character interpretations.

Exercises to Sharpen Your Observation Skills:

1. People-Watching: This timeless practice is your go-to tool. Choose a public space like a park, café, or station, and simply observe people. Focus on:

- ***Body Language:*** Notice postures, gestures, facial expressions, and how they communicate emotions and intentions.
- ***Interactions:*** Observe how people interact with each other, their verbal and nonverbal cues, and the dynamics within groups.
- ***Emotional Expressions:*** Pay attention to how people express joy, sadness, anger, or nervousness through their movements and expressions.

2. Character Studies: Select a specific character from a film, book, or even real life. Analyze their:

- ***Physical Characteristics:*** Height, posture, gait, mannerisms, and unique physical details.

- ***Speech Patterns:*** Accents, vocal inflections, word choices, and how they speak under pressure.
- ***Emotional Range:*** Observe how they express different emotions and the specific behaviour associated with each emotion.

3. Mirror Work: Observe people while practicing mirroring their posture, gestures, and facial expressions subtly. This deepens your understanding of nonverbal communication and how it connects to emotions.

4. Sensory Immersion: Choose a specific setting from a play or film. Imagine yourself there. What do you see, hear, smell, and feel? Allow these sensory details to inform your physicality and emotional responses.

5. Emotional Recall: Pick a strong emotional memory from your life. Practice recalling it vividly while performing a monologue or scene. Observe how accessing genuine emotions impacts your delivery and presence.

Beyond the Basics:

- ***Expand Your Focus:*** Observe not just individuals but also group dynamics, cultural nuances, and the environment itself.
- ***Be Specific:*** Don't just collect generic observations; focus on specific details that paint a vivid picture for your characters.
- ***Analyze and Apply:*** Reflect on your observations and see how they connect to specific characters you're working on.

- ***Embrace Diversity:*** Observe people from different backgrounds, ages, and social groups to enrich your understanding of human behavior.

Remember: Observation is a lifelong journey. The more you practice, the more you become a keen observer, enriching your character portrayals and igniting your creative process. Don't just watch; see, analyze, and use your observations to unlock the power of authentic acting.

Bonus Tip: Watch documentaries and films known for their realistic portrayals. Analyze how actors use observation to bring their characters to life.

---------- **End of Chapter 4** ----------

CHAPTER 5: Imagination
Unleashing Creativity in Acting

Theory:

Imagine stepping into the shoes of a pirate captain, a heartbroken lover, or a mischievous alien. As an actor, your imagination is your passport to countless worlds and experiences. It fuels character development, allows you to dive deep into scenes, and empowers you to improvise with confidence. So, unlock your creative mind and embark on a journey to unleash your imagination's true potential.

Why Imagination Matters:

- ***Character Development:*** Your imagination breathes life into characters. Use it to create their backstory, fears, desires, and unique quirks. Imagine their childhood memories, deepest secrets, and how they react in unexpected situations.
- ***Scene Analysis:*** Don't just read the script; imagine it. Picture the setting vividly, envision the characters' interactions, and feel the emotional charge of each scene. This analysis builds a deeper understanding and unlocks hidden layers of meaning.

- ***Improvisation:*** When faced with unexpected prompts or scenarios, your imagination saves the day. It allows you to react spontaneously, invent details on the fly, and create believable responses that keep the scene alive.
- ***Emotional Connection:*** Going beyond memorizing lines, imagine the emotions your character feels. Picture yourself in their shoes, facing their challenges and experiencing their joys. This fuels genuine emotional expression and connects you to the character's core.

Exercises to Unleash Your Imagination:

1. Sensory Journeys: Choose a scene from a play or film. Close your eyes and imagine yourself there. Focus on your five senses:

- ***Sight:*** What do you see? Describe the environment, costumes, and characters in detail.
- ***Sound:*** What do you hear? Dialogue, background noise, even your own heartbeat.
- ***Smell:*** Are there specific scents in the air? Use your imagination to create unique sensory details.
- ***Touch:*** What textures do you feel? The roughness of a wooden table, the softness of a silk dress.
- ***Taste:*** Is there a taste associated with the scene? Imagine it vividly.

2. Character Backstory: Choose a character you're working on. Imagine their life before the play or film begins. Where did they grow up? What are their hidden dreams and fears? Create a detailed backstory that informs their present behavior.

3. "What If" Scenarios: Take a scene from a script and explore alternate possibilities. What if the character received unexpected news? What if they reacted differently to a situation? Improvise based on these "what ifs" and explore the scene's hidden potential.

4. Emotional Exploration: Pick a strong emotion like joy, fear, or anger. Find a quiet space and close your eyes. Imagine yourself experiencing that emotion intensely. Focus on your physical sensations, thoughts, and facial expressions. Use this experience to inform your emotional portrayal in scenes.

5. "People-Watching" with Imagination: Observe people around you, but go beyond their physical appearance. Imagine their inner world – their hopes, dreams, and hidden stories. Invent details about their lives and use them to fuel your own creative writing or character building.

Beyond the Basics:

- ***Challenge Yourself:*** Don't limit yourself to familiar scenarios. Push your imagination by exploring bizarre situations, exotic settings, and complex emotions.
- ***Practice Regularly:*** Like a muscle, your imagination needs exercise. Engage in daily exercises, improvise regularly, and keep your creative spark alive.

- ***Find Inspiration:*** Seek inspiration from art, music, literature, and nature. Allow these experiences to fuel your imagination and spark new ideas.

Remember: Imagination is not just about fantastical worlds; it's about bringing depth and authenticity to every role you play. By unlocking your imagination's power, you become a more versatile, engaging, and ultimately, a more captivating actor.

Bonus Tip: Watch actors known for their strong improvisational skills. Analyze how they use their imagination to create believable characters and react spontaneously in scenes.

---------- **End of Chapter 5** ----------

<u>**PART 2: BUILDING YOUR CHARACTER**</u>

CHAPTER 6: Deciphering Emotions
The Actor's Palette of Expression

Theory:

As an actor, your ability to express emotions authentically is the lifeblood of your craft. It's not just about memorizing lines and hitting marks; it's about inhabiting your character's soul, navigating the vast landscape of human experience, and translating it into performances that resonate with audiences on a deep level. This chapter delves into the intricacies of emotions, providing you with the tools to decipher their complexities and translate them into truthful, captivating expressions.

Understanding the Emotional Landscape:

Emotions are far from one-dimensional. While out of 9 rasas in Natyashasatra, the basic six – joy, sadness, anger, fear, surprise, and disgust – form the foundation, countless nuances and combinations paint the full picture. Mastering them requires understanding:

- *Intensity:* Emotions exist on a spectrum, ranging from the fleeting flutter of amusement to the crushing weight of grief. Identifying the appropriate intensity is crucial for believable expression.
- *Authenticity:* Each individual experiences emotion differently. Avoid clichés or overacting; strive for genuine expression that reflects your character's unique inner world.
- *Physical Manifestations:* Emotions are intricately linked to our bodies. Understanding the physical manifestations – changes in posture, facial expressions, vocal qualities – is vital for conveying them authentically.
- *Context and Triggers:* Emotions rarely arise in isolation. Consider the scene's context and your character's internal triggers to understand what sparks the emotion and how it manifests.

Delving into the Nuances:

Let's explore some key emotions and how to bring them to life:

1. Joy:

- *Physicality:* Relaxed posture, open body language, upward smiles, sparkling eyes, genuine laughter (varying intensity and duration).
- *Vocal Qualities:* Lively tone, increased pace, animated speech, playful inflections.
- *Exercises:* Recall a joyful memory, physically embody joy through movement, practice mirroring expressions of joy in others, improvise scenarios with joyful discoveries or reunions.

2. Sadness:

- *Physicality:* Slumped posture, downcast eyes, trembling lips, slow movements, hesitant gestures.
- *Vocal Qualities:* Quieter tone, slower pace, broken voice, sniffles (if appropriate), pauses between words.
- *Exercises:* Write down words associated with sadness, imagine yourself experiencing different degrees of sadness (grief, disappointment, loneliness), practice conveying specific nuances through facial expressions and vocal variations.

3. Anger:

- *Physicality:* Tense posture, clenched fists, furrowed brows, flushed cheeks, dilated pupils.
- *Vocal Qualities:* Raised tone, faster pace, sharp words, growling (controlled and purposeful).
- *Exercises:* Recall an experience that made you angry, practice expressing different levels of anger (frustration, rage, righteous indignation), use

physical exercises to release tension before performing.

4. Fear:

- *Physicality:* Wide eyes, frozen posture, shallow breaths, trembling hands, jerky movements.
- *Vocal Qualities:* Stuttering, shaky voice, high-pitched gasps or screams (used sparingly), stammering.
- *Exercises:* Watch suspenseful films, imagine facing your own fears (public speaking, heights), practice conveying different types of fear (panic, apprehension, terror).

5. Surprise:

- *Physicality:* Raised eyebrows, open mouth, momentary freeze, hands flying up, dropped jaw.
- *Vocal Qualities:* Gasp, quick intake of breath, stammering, surprised yelps or shouts (depending on the situation).
- *Exercises:* Practice reacting to unexpected sounds or events, improvise scenarios with sudden surprises, record yourself reacting genuinely to surprises.

Exercises for Deeper Exploration:

- *Emotional Spectrum Chart:* Create a chart listing various emotions and their physical, vocal, and internal manifestations. Fill it in for specific characters you're working on, noting their unique traits and cultural background.

- ***Emotional Monologues:*** Choose monologues with complex emotional journeys. Analyze the character's emotions at each stage and practice expressing them truthfully, incorporating physicality and vocal variations.
- ***Mirror Work with Emotions:*** Watch yourself in the mirror while expressing different emotions. Pay attention to your physicality and vocal qualities, and adjust as needed

Beyond the Basics:

- ***Emotional Blending:*** Emotions rarely exist in isolation. Combine joy with relief, anger with frustration, to create complex and realistic portrayals.
- ***Observing the Real World:*** Watch how people express emotions in everyday life. Notice subtle cues, cultural differences, and individual variations to inform your performances.
- ***Exploring Cultural Nuances:*** Different cultures have unique ways of expressing emotions. Be mindful of the specific context and cultural cues of your character.
- ***Go Beyond Forced Expressions:*** Emotions should flow naturally from the character and scene. Avoid forcing expressions or relying solely on external cues.

Remember: Exploring emotions is a lifelong journey. Embrace the complexities, experiment, and don't be afraid to make mistakes. With dedication and practice, you'll unlock the true power of emotions in your performances, captivating audiences and leaving a lasting impact.

Bonus Tip: Watch interviews with actors discussing their approach to expressing emotions. Analyze their insights and connect them to the techniques discussed in this chapter.

---------- **End of Chapter 6** ----------

CHAPTER 7: Bringing Words to Life
Mastering the Power of Speech

Theory:

As an actor, your voice is your instrument, and words your paintbrush. But simply memorizing lines isn't enough. To truly captivate audiences, you need to master the art of diction, articulation, and textual analysis, transforming words into impactful performances. This chapter guides you through this essential journey, equipping you with the tools to breathe life into every syllable and deliver text with meaning and power.

The Power of Diction:

Words are more than just sounds; they carry meaning, weight, and intent. Choosing the right word, with its specific nuance and emotional undertone, paints a vivid picture for the audience. Consider:

- ***Specificity:*** Opt for precise, evocative words that paint a clear picture rather than generic descriptors. "Crimson" evokes a different image than "red."
- ***Subtext:*** Words often carry hidden meanings beyond their literal definition. Delve into the subtext to understand the character's true message and motivations.
- ***Emotional Impact:*** Consider the emotional weight of your words. Are they meant to be playful, sarcastic, passionate, or melancholic? Choose words that convey the intended emotion.

Exercises to Sharpen Your Diction:

- ***Word Games:*** Engage in word association games, thesaurus exploration, and synonym challenges to expand your vocabulary and discover specific, evocative words.
- ***Script Analysis:*** Analyze the script, identifying words with multiple meanings, potential subtext, and emotional nuances. Write down synonyms and explore their impact on the scene.
- ***Monologue Makeovers:*** Choose a monologue and rewrite it using more specific, evocative words while maintaining the original meaning. Observe the shift in meaning and emotional impact.

The Art of Articulation:

Clear and impactful delivery is crucial for connecting with your audience. Mastering articulation entails:

- ***Pronunciation:*** Ensure crisp pronunciation of each syllable, avoiding mumbling or unclear sounds. Practice tongue twisters and diction exercises to improve clarity.
- ***Projection:*** Find your vocal power without shouting. Practice projecting your voice naturally to reach the back of the room without losing emotion.
- ***Pace and Rhythm:*** Vary your pace and rhythm to avoid monotony. Use slow delivery for emphasis and faster speech for urgency or excitement.
- ***Pauses and Punctuation:*** Respect punctuation, but also use strategic pauses to add meaning and emotional depth. Silence can be as powerful as words.

Exercises to Master Articulation:

- ***Tongue Twisters:*** Regularly practice tongue twisters to improve enunciation and articulation. Start slow and gradually increase speed while maintaining clarity.
- ***Text Reading:*** Read aloud from various genres, focusing on clear pronunciation, proper breathing, and varied pacing. Record yourself and identify areas for improvement.
- ***Mirror Work:*** Practice delivering lines in front of a mirror, paying attention to your mouth and jaw movements. Ensure clear articulation and avoid excessive movements.

Deeper Text Analysis: Unlocking Meaning:

A script is more than just lines; it's a blueprint for understanding your character and their journey. Effective textual analysis involves:

- ***Subtext and Intent:*** Analyze the subtext behind each line, considering your character's true emotions, motivations, and hidden agendas.
- ***Internal Monologue:*** Imagine your character's internal monologue – their unspoken thoughts and feelings – to inform your delivery and choices.
- ***Context and Relationships:*** Understand the scene's context, your character's relationship with others, and how these factors influence their delivery of lines.

Exercises for Deeper Analysis:

- ***Character Backstory:*** Develop a detailed backstory for your character, including their thoughts, fears, and desires. Use this backstory to inform your interpretation of the text.
- ***Scene Breakdown:*** Break down each scene, identifying your character's objectives, challenges, and emotional shifts. Analyze how the text reflects these elements.
- ***Improvisation:*** Based on your textual analysis, improvise scenes exploring different interpretations of the script and your character's choices.

Beyond the Basics:

- ***Listen and Learn:*** Observe skilled actors deliver dialogue. Pay attention to their diction, articulation, and how they bring text to life.
- ***Embrace Accents and Dialects:*** Explore different accents and dialects to expand your range and enhance character portrayals. Ensure authenticity and avoid stereotypes.
- ***Record and Reflect:*** Record yourself performing scenes and monologues. Listen back critically to identify areas for improvement in diction, articulation, and textual understanding.

Remember: Mastering diction, articulation, and textual analysis is a lifelong pursuit. With dedication and practice, you'll unlock the true power of speech, transforming script lines into captivating performances that resonate with audiences and leave a lasting impact.

Bonus Tip: Watch interviews with actors discussing their approach to text analysis and vocal preparation. Analyze their insights and connect them to the techniques discussed in this chapter.

---------- End of Chapter 7 --------

CHAPTER 8: Embodying the Character:
Transforming Through
Costume, Makeup & Physicality

Theory:

As an actor, your physical presence is an essential storytelling tool. Beyond memorizing lines and delivering them with conviction, you have the power to embody your character through their outward expression. This chapter delves into the transformative power of costume, makeup, and physicality, guiding you to use them as extensions of your character's inner world and connect with audiences on a deeper level.

Understanding the Power of Transformation:

- *Costume:* Clothing isn't just fabric; it tells a story. Consider the character's socioeconomic status, personality, and background when choosing a costume. Does it reflect their profession, values, or even their current emotional state?
- *Makeup:* Makeup can subtly enhance or dramatically transform your appearance. Use it to highlight physical characteristics, convey age, social status, or even suggest a specific mood or emotion.
- *Physicality:* Your posture, movement, and gestures speak volumes about your character. Consider their physical attributes, personality traits, and emotional state to create a believable physical embodiment.

Unlocking the Magic of Costume:

- ***Research and Inspiration:*** Immerse yourself in research related to your character's time period, social class, and cultural background. Look at historical photographs, paintings, and films for inspiration.
- ***Beyond the Basics:*** Pay attention to details like fabric textures, colours, and accessories. Do they tell a story about your character's personality, occupation, or hidden desires?
- ***Collaboration is Key:*** Work closely with costume designers to ensure your vision aligns with the director's interpretation of the character. Don't be afraid to suggest adjustments to truly embody your character.

Exercises for Costume Exploration:

- ***Character Collage:*** Create a collage of images showcasing different costume options for your character. Consider different eras, styles, and accessories, and explain how they reflect your understanding of the character.
- ***Costuming Historical Figures:*** Research a historical figure and recreate their attire using readily available materials. Analyze how the costume choices inform your portrayal.
- ***Costume Swap:*** Exchange costumes with another actor and embody a character completely different from your own. Analyze how the costume impacts your physicality and emotional approach.

The Art of Makeup: Enhancing Your Portrayal:

- ***Less is More:*** Subtlety is key. Avoid over-the-top makeup that distracts from your performance. Use it to enhance your features and reflect your character's personality or background.
- ***Research and Inspiration:*** Look at historical makeup trends, specific cultural practices, or even individual portraits for inspiration depending on your character.
- ***Practice Makes Perfect:*** Experiment with different makeup techniques and products before applying them on stage or camera. Ensure you feel comfortable and confident in your character's transformed appearance.

Exercises for Makeup Exploration:

- ***Character Sketches:*** Draw different versions of your character with varying makeup styles. Consider how each look affects the overall portrayal and the message it conveys.
- ***Historical Makeup Research:*** Choose a specific historical period and research its makeup trends. Attempt to recreate a look from that era, analyzing its challenges and how it affects your performance.
- ***No-Makeup Challenge:*** Perform a scene without any makeup. Observe how your physicality and emotional expression shift in the absence of external enhancements.

Embodying the Character through Physicality:

- *Movement and Posture:* Consider your character's physical attributes, age, occupation, and emotional state. How would these factors influence their posture, gait, and movement?
- *Gesture and Mannerisms:* Observe subtle gestures and mannerisms specific to your character's background or personality. How do they fidget, hold themselves, or react to situations?
- *Voice and Physicality:* Remember, your voice is part of your physical expression. Consider how your character's physicality might influence their vocal qualities, pitch, and speech patterns.

Exercises for Physicality Exploration:

- *Animal Studies:* Observe the movement and behavior of different animals. Adapt specific aspects of their physicality to inform your character's movement language.
- *Mirror Work:* Practice embodying your character in front of a mirror, observing your posture, gestures, and facial expressions. Adjust them to align with your interpretation of the character.
- *Shadow Work:* Have another actor observe you from behind, providing feedback on your posture, movement, and overall physical embodiment of the character.

Beyond the Basics:

- ***Collaborate with Other Departments:*** Work closely with directors, movement coaches, and makeup artists to ensure your costume, makeup, and physicality choices are cohesive and support the overall vision of the production.
- ***Observe and Adapt:*** Pay attention to how people around you move and express themselves. Adapt specific elements to create unique and believable physical portrayals.
- ***Stay Authentic:*** Don't rely solely on external elements; ensure your physicality is driven by your character's inner

Remember: Costume, makeup, and physicality are collaborative processes that involve input from directors, designers, and fellow actors. Stay open to feedback and be willing to adjust your approach based on the vision of the creative team. Trust in the collective effort to bring the character to life.

Bonus Tip: Take photographs or videos of yourself in costume and makeup during rehearsals. Reviewing them can provide valuable insights into your character's physical transformation and help refine your performance.

---------- **End of Chapter 8** ----------

CHAPTER 9: Developing Your Instrument
Honing Your Craft Through
Vocal and Physical Exercises

Theory:

As an actor, your body and voice are your instruments, the tools you use to breathe life into characters and captivate audiences. But just like any instrument, they require consistent practice and refinement to reach their full potential. This chapter equips you with a range of vocal and physical exercises to strengthen your abilities, deepen your understanding of your instrument, and ultimately elevate your acting to new heights.

Understanding the Actor's Instrument:

Imagine your body and voice as an orchestra – capable of expressing a vast array of emotions, dynamics, and nuances. Your voice becomes the melody, conveying meaning and intention, while your body serves as the rhythm, reflecting your character's physicality and emotional state. Both aspects require dedicated practice to achieve mastery.

The Power of Vocal Exercises:

- *Vocal Warm-ups:* Just like athletes, your voice needs a warm-up to avoid strain and ensure optimal performance. Regular practice of vocal scales, lip trills, and humming exercises improves flexibility, range, and projection.
- *Articulation and Pronunciation:* Master the clear and precise delivery of syllables. Practice tongue twisters, read aloud from diverse texts, and record yourself to identify areas for improvement.
- *Breathing Techniques:* Effective breath control is essential for dynamic vocal delivery. Exercises like diaphragmatic breathing and sustained inhalations help you project your voice clearly and maintain vocal stamina.
- *Emotional Expression:* Explore how emotions affect your vocal qualities. Practice delivering lines with different emotions, adjusting pitch, pace, and vocal texture to convey genuine expression.

Vocal Exercises for Every Actor:

- *Alphabet Sounds:* Pronounce each letter of the alphabet slowly and exaggeratedly, focusing on clear articulation and resonance.
- *Tongue Twisters:* Choose classic tongue twisters like "Peter Piper picked a peck of pickled peppers" and gradually increase your speed while maintaining clarity.

- ***Mirror Work:*** Practice delivering monologues while observing your facial expressions and mouth movements. Ensure your articulation matches your vocal intent.
- ***Textual Exploration:*** Read aloud from varied genres, focusing on capturing the author's intended emotions and adapting your voice accordingly.
- ***Emotional Spectrum:*** Write down a list of emotions and practice expressing each through varying vocal qualities (pitch, pace, volume).

The Importance of Physical Training:

- ***Body Awareness:*** Develop a deep understanding of your body through movement exercises, yoga, or dance classes. Improve your proprioception and control over your physical expression.
- ***Neutral Posture:*** Master a neutral, aligned posture as the foundation for all character portrayals. Practice standing tall, engaging your core, and releasing unnecessary tension.
- ***Movement Exploration:*** Explore different movement styles – mime, animal studies, improvisation – to expand your physical vocabulary and create unique character portrayals.
- ***Stage Combat and Movement:*** Consider training in stage combat or movement techniques specific to your acting goals. These skills can enhance your physical presence and confidence on stage.

Physical Exercises to Ignite Your Performance:

- *Animal Imitations:* Observe the movement and posture of different animals and practice embodying them. Analyze how their physicality translates to emotional expression.
- *Mirror Walks:* Walk across the room with varying emotions (joy, anger, sadness) while observing your posture, gait, and physical energy.
- *Improvisation Games:* Participate in improvisation games that require physical expression and storytelling. Adapt your movement to reflect the changing scenarios and emotions.
- *Shadow Work:* Have another actor observe you move silently, providing feedback on your physical storytelling and emotional expression.
- *Stage Combat Basics:* Learn basic stage combat techniques to safely and convincingly portray physical altercations on stage.

Beyond the Basics:

- *Consistency is Key:* Integrate vocal and physical exercises into your daily routine for sustained improvement.
- *Find a Mentor:* Consider working with a vocal coach or movement specialist to receive personalized feedback and guidance.
- *Embrace Challenges*: Step outside your comfort zone and explore new vocal and physical techniques to expand your range and challenge your abilities.

- ***Observe and Adapt:*** Pay attention to skilled actors and analyze their vocal and physical choices. Adapt elements to your own approach while maintaining your individuality.

Remember: Developing your instrument is a lifelong journey. Embrace the process, celebrate your growth, and never stop exploring. With dedication and practice, you'll unlock the full potential of your voice and body, transforming them into powerful tools for storytelling and captivating audiences with your performances.

Bonus Tip: Watch interviews with actors discussing their personal approaches to vocal and physical training. Analyze their insights and connect them to the exercises discussed in this chapter.

---------- **End of Chapter 9** ----------

CHAPTER 10: Focus and Concentration
The Actor's Spotlight in the Storm

Theory:

As an actor, you step onto the stage or set – a world of its own, filled with distractions, emotions, and demanding expectations. Maintaining focus amidst this swirling storm is crucial for delivering powerful, believable performances. This chapter delves into the art of concentration, providing tools and techniques to sharpen your mental clarity and ensure you shine brightly under pressure.

Understanding the Art of Focus:

Focus is not just about staring intently; it's about actively engaging your mind and shutting out distractions. It allows you to fully inhabit your character, respond authentically to your scene partners, and connect deeply with the audience.

Challenges to Concentration:

- ***Internal Distractions:*** Self-doubt, nerves, and emotional baggage can pull your focus away from the present moment. Techniques to manage these internal hurdles are essential.
- ***External Distractions:*** Stage lights, noises, audience movements – these external elements can disrupt your concentration if not acknowledged and managed effectively.
- ***Breaking Character:*** Staying in character throughout the performance requires laser-sharp focus to avoid breaking out and losing the emotional thread.

Sharpening Your Mental Spotlight:

- ***Meditation and Mindfulness:*** Cultivate present-moment awareness through meditation practices. This helps manage distracting thoughts and emotions, improving your ability to focus on the now.
- ***Visualization:*** Visualize yourself delivering a focused, powerful performance. Imagine the feeling of being fully present and in control, boosting your confidence and mental preparation.
- ***Positive Affirmations:*** Counteract negative self-talk with positive affirmations about your abilities and focus. Repeating statements like "I am present" or "I am focused" can quiet anxieties and enhance your confidence.

Exercises for Laser-Sharp Focus:

- ***Five Senses Grounding:*** When distracted, engage each of your five senses in the present moment. Describe in detail what you see, hear, smell, taste, and touch. This refocuses your attention on the immediate environment.
- ***Counting Exercise:*** Choose a simple object onstage and slowly count its individual parts out loud. This mentally anchors you in the present moment and reduces distractions.
- ***Improvisation with Distractions:*** Practice improvising scenes while incorporating planned distractions (loud noises, unexpected movements). Adapt and maintain focus, learning to overcome external challenges.

Maintaining Focus in Character:

- ***Emotional Anchors:*** Identify key emotional moments in your character's journey. Mentally rehearse these moments, connecting them to physical sensations and memories to recall them easily onstage.
- ***Staying in the "Scene Bubble":*** Imagine an invisible bubble around your character and scene. Focus on what happens within the bubble, minimizing awareness of external distractions.
- ***Breathing Techniques***: Controlled breathing helps manage nervous energy and maintain focus. Practice diaphragmatic breathing to stay calm and present in the moment.

Beyond the Basics:

- ***Warm-up Rituals:*** Develop pre-performance routines that calm your mind and prepare you for focused acting. This could include meditation, light exercises, or listening to calming music.
- ***Healthy Habits:*** Ensure adequate sleep, hydration, and nutritious meals. Taking care of your physical well-being improves your mental clarity and concentration.
- ***Celebrate Progress:*** Acknowledge your improvements in focus and celebrate your ability to overcome distractions. This positive reinforcement motivates you to continue honing your mental resilience.

Remember: Maintaining focus is a continuous journey, not a destination. Embrace the challenges, experiment with different techniques, and trust your ability to grow. With dedication and practice, you'll develop the laser-sharp concentration needed to deliver captivating performances, leaving audiences mesmerized by your presence and story.

Bonus Tip: Watch interviews with actors discussing their strategies for managing distractions and maintaining focus on stage. Analyze their insights and incorporate them into your own toolbox.

---------- **End of Chapter 10** ----------

CHAPTER 11: Creating Connection:
Building Bridges and Sharing the Spotlight

Theory:

As an actor, you don't exist in a vacuum on stage. Your performance thrives on the connections you forge with your fellow actors, creating a tapestry of shared experiences that resonates with the audience. This chapter delves into the art of building genuine relationships and navigating the dynamics of the stage, transforming your interactions into powerful storytelling tools.

Understanding the Power of Connection:

Actors aren't just delivering lines; they're weaving a web of relationships, each interaction shaping the narrative and emotional landscape of the play. True connection goes beyond memorizing lines; it involves active listening, responding authentically, and building trust with your scene partners.

Building Bridges of Trust and Understanding:

- *Active Listening:* Be fully present, listen deeply to your scene partners, and truly hear their emotional undertones. Respond not just to words, but to the unspoken emotions behind them.

- ***Collaboration and Communication:*** Acting is a collaborative art. Openly communicate with your scene partners, discuss character interpretations, and work together to create a unified vision for the scene.
- ***Respect and Empathy:*** Treat your fellow actors with respect, both on and off stage. Cultivate empathy for their characters and understand their motivations, fostering genuine connection.

Exercises to Build Strong Bonds:

- ***Character Backstory Exploration:*** Share your character's backstory and motivations with your scene partners. Encourage them to do the same, fostering deeper understanding and connection.
- ***Improvisation Games:*** Engage in improvisation games that require collaboration, trust, and active listening. These exercises build rapport and sharpen your ability to respond authentically.
- ***Emotional Exchange:*** Choose a scene with strong emotional content. Practice delivering lines while focusing solely on conveying your character's emotions to your scene partner, without words.

Navigating Stage Dynamics:

The stage is a dynamic space, filled with unspoken rules and unspoken language. Understanding these dynamics allows you to navigate them seamlessly, enhancing your performance and enriching your connection with your scene partners.

- ***Stage Awareness:*** Be mindful of your position on stage relative to your scene partners and the audience. Use blocking and movement strategically to convey power dynamics, intimacy, or emotional shifts.
- ***Eyeline and Focus:*** Maintain eye contact and focus on your scene partners, not the audience. This creates a sense of shared reality and strengthens the emotional connection.
- ***Energetic Exchange:*** Match the energy of your scene partners. Respond to their emotional intensity, adjust your own energy accordingly, and create a captivating push and pull between characters.

Exercises for Stage Dynamics:

- ***Mirror Work:*** Practice scenes with a partner, mirroring their movements and expressions. This fosters a sense of connection and helps you respond instinctively.
- ***Non-Verbal Communication:*** Perform a scene without speaking, relying solely on facial expressions, gestures, and movement to convey emotions and relationships.
- ***Space Exploration:*** Explore different spatial relationships with your scene partners on stage.

- Observe how proximity, body angles, and movement impact the perceived power dynamics and emotional connection.

Beyond the Basics:

- ***Observe and Learn:*** Watch skilled actors interact on stage. Analyze their use of eye contact, body language, and energetic exchange to create believable connections.
- ***Embrace Vulnerability***: Don't be afraid to be vulnerable and share your emotions authentically on stage. True connection often arises from shared vulnerability.
- ***Celebrate Each Other:*** Acknowledge and celebrate the contributions of your fellow actors. This fosters a positive and collaborative environment where everyone thrives.

Remember: Building genuine connections and understanding stage dynamics is an ongoing process. Embrace the journey, experiment, and never stop learning. With dedication and practice, you'll transform your interactions into powerful storytelling tools, weaving a web of connection that captivates audiences and leaves a lasting impact.

Bonus Tip: Watch interviews with actors discussing their experiences building connections on stage and navigating stage dynamics. Analyze their insights and incorporate them into your own approach.

--------- End of Chapter 11 ----------

CHAPTER 12: Living in the Moment
Embracing the Flow and Reacting Authentically

Theory:

As an actor, you step onto the stage, lines memorized, emotions prepared. But scripts are blueprints, not rigid maps. The magic truly happens when you let go of rigidity and embrace the present moment, reacting authentically to your scene partners and the unexpected twists and turns that unfold. This chapter delves into the art of living in the moment, shedding the constraints of overthinking and cultivating the spontaneity that fuels captivating performances.

Understanding the Power of Presence:

Unlike film, theatre is a living, breathing entity. Each performance is unique, shaped by the interplay of actors, audience energy, and even unforeseen circumstances. Living in the moment allows you to tap into this dynamic flow, responding authentically to every nuance and creating a truly captivating experience.

The Pitfalls of Overthinking:

Clinging to scripted lines and pre-planned emotions restricts your ability to truly inhabit your character. Overthinking stifles spontaneity, leaving your performance sterile and predictable. Embrace the present moment and allow yourself to be surprised, both by your scene partners and your own emotional responses.

Cultivating Spontaneity and Authenticity:

- *Trust Your Instincts:* Don't overanalyze every beat. Learn to trust your instincts and react emotionally to what's happening in the moment. Let your character respond intuitively to the scene's unfolding circumstances.
- *Active Listening and Responding:* Be present for your scene partners, listening not just to words but to their non-verbal cues and emotional subtext. Respond instinctively, allowing their energy to influence your own performance.
- *Embrace the Unexpected:* Mistakes happen, lines get forgotten, and props malfunction. Instead of panicking, embrace the unexpected! Use these moments to improvise, adapt, and stay true to your character's reaction in the present situation.

Exercises to Sharpen Your Presence:

- *Improvisation Games:* Engage in improvisation games that require quick thinking and spontaneous reactions. These exercises train your mind to respond instinctively and overcome the fear of the unknown.

- ***Sensory Exploration:*** Close your eyes and focus on your senses. Describe in detail what you hear, smell, taste, and touch. This practice grounds you in the present moment and heightens your awareness of your surroundings.
- ***Mirror Work with Emotions:*** Practice delivering monologues while focusing on embodying different emotions authentically. Pay attention to how your body and voice naturally respond to each emotion.

Embracing the "Yes, And" Mentality:

In improv, the golden rule is "Yes, And." Rather than negating or blocking your scene partner's ideas, build upon them, adding your own spontaneous contributions. This collaborative approach fosters a dynamic flow and encourages genuine connection on stage.

Exercises for "Yes, And":

- ***Scene Continuation:*** Start a scene with a simple prompt and take turns adding improvisational lines, building upon each other's ideas and creating a collaborative narrative.
- ***Object Transformation:*** Choose an object and take turns improvising scenes, each person using the object in a different, unexpected way. Embrace the absurdity and spontaneity.
- ***Character Exchanges:*** Start a scene with one character, then switch roles seamlessly within the scene, continuing the story from the other

character's perspective. Adapt and react authentically to the change.

Beyond the Basics:

- ***Observe Life:*** Pay attention to how people interact in everyday life. Observe their spontaneous reactions, emotional shifts, and nonverbal cues. Use these observations to enrich your portrayal of characters.
- ***Silence is Powerful:*** Don't feel obligated to fill every pause with words. Embrace the power of silence, allowing it to add depth and emotional weight to your performance.
- ***Let Go of Perfectionism:*** Let go of the need for perfection and allow yourself to be present in the moment, flaws and all.

Remember: Living in the moment is a journey, not a destination. Embrace the challenges, experiment with different techniques, and trust your ability to connect with your scene partners and the audience. With dedication and practice, you'll unlock the magic of spontaneity, transforming your performances into truly breathtaking, authentic experiences that resonate long after the curtain falls.

Bonus Tip: Watch interviews with actors discussing their experiences embracing spontaneity and living in the moment on stage. Analyze their insights and incorporate them into your own approach.

---------- **End of Chapter 12** ----------

CHAPTER 13: Projecting Your Energy:
Commanding the Stage or Screen with Confidence and Presence

Theory:

Stepping onto the stage or setting your gaze on the camera lens can be daunting. Yet, captivating performances require more than just delivering lines; they demand the ability to project your energy, captivate the audience, and command attention through confident stage presence. This chapter delves into the secrets of effective projection, empowering you to radiate confidence and connect with your audience on a deeper level.

Understanding the Power of Projection:

Projection is more than just volume; it's the art of transmitting your character's emotions, intentions, and inner world through your entire being – voice, body, and emotional engagement. Effective projection allows you to fill the space, hold the audience's attention, and deliver your performance with clarity and impact.

The Pitfalls of Weak Projection:

Mumbling, hesitant delivery, and lack of eye contact create a barrier between you and the audience. They struggle to hear you, connect with your character, and fully immerse themselves in the story. Strong projection breaks down these barriers, leaving audiences engaged and invested in your journey.

Building Your Stage Presence:

- *Vocal Techniques:* Master breath control, projection exercises, and clear articulation to ensure your voice carries and resonates. Practice speaking with conviction and varying your vocal dynamics to express emotions effectively.
- *Physicality and Posture:* Stand tall, engage your core, and radiate confidence through your posture. Utilize expressive gestures and purposeful movement to enhance your storytelling and convey character traits.
- *Eye Contact and Connection:* Make genuine eye contact with your scene partners and the audience. This creates a connection, draws them into the scene, and conveys your character's emotions and intentions directly.

Exercises to Amplify Your Projection:

- *Vocal Warm-ups:* Dedicate time daily to vocal warm-up exercises like scales, tongue twisters, and humming. This improves vocal flexibility, projection, and clarity.

- ***Mirror Work:*** Practice monologues and scenes while observing your posture, gestures, and eye contact. Adjust them to project confidence and embody your character authentically.
- ***Improv with Focus:*** Participate in improvisation exercises that require strong communication and audience engagement. This improves your ability to think on your feet and project your voice and energy effectively.

Developing Emotional Connection:

Projection isn't just about shouting louder; it's about conveying genuine emotions that resonate with the audience. Tap into your character's inner world and allow your emotions to shine through your voice, body language, and facial expressions.

Exercises to Spark Emotional Connection:

- ***Emotional Recall:*** Choose a scene with strong emotional content. Close your eyes and vividly recall a personal experience that evokes similar emotions. Replay the emotions as you deliver the scene, allowing them to fuel your performance.
- ***Sensory Exploration:*** Imagine yourself in your character's shoes. Describe in detail the sights, sounds, smells, and textures surrounding them. Let these sensory details inform your physicality and emotional expression.
- ***Character Object:*** Choose an object significant to your character and hold it throughout the scene. Let the object connect you to your character's

memories, emotions, and motivations, influencing your projection and behaviour.

Beyond the Basics:

- ***Confidence is Key:*** Believe in yourself and your ability to captivate the audience. Confidence radiates through your performance and helps you overcome stage fright.
- ***Observe and Learn:*** Watch skilled actors and analyze how they project their energy and connect with the audience. Adapt their techniques and incorporate them into your own toolbox.
- ***Embrace Vulnerability:*** Don't be afraid to be vulnerable and share your emotions authentically on stage. True connection often arises from shared vulnerability and heartfelt performances.

Remember: Projecting your energy is a continuous process, not a one-time achievement. Embrace the journey, experiment with different techniques, and never stop refining your stage presence. With dedication and practice, you'll illuminate the stage or screen with captivating energy, leaving audiences mesmerized and deeply moved by your performances.

Bonus Tip: Record yourself performing scenes and watch them back critically. Analyze your projection, vocal clarity, and stage presence. Identify areas for improvement and practice targeted exercises to address them.

---------- **End of Chapter 13** ---------

CHAPTER 14: Internalization and Truth
Diving Deep to Discover Your Character's Soul

Theory:

As an actor, your journey doesn't begin with memorizing lines. It starts with delving into the heart of your character, uncovering their desires, fears, and the invisible threads that weave their very existence. This chapter serves as a guide to internalization, equipping you with techniques to unlock your character's inner truth and deliver performances that resonate on a profound emotional level.

Beyond the Script: Understanding Internalization:

Internalization is not just memorizing lines and blocking. It's a transformative process where you inhabit your character's skin, understand their motivations, and connect with their emotional core. This allows you to deliver lines not just as words, but as genuine expressions of your character's inner world.

Why Embrace Internalization?

- ***Depth and Authenticity:*** By truly knowing your character, you transcend mere recitation and breathe life into their actions, reactions, and emotions. The audience witnesses not just a performance, but the unfolding of a complex human being.

- ***Emotional Connection:*** When you're deeply connected to your character's truth, your emotions flow naturally. This emotional authenticity resonates with the audience, drawing them into your character's journey and sparking a deeper connection.
- ***Improvisation and Adaptation:*** Internalization empowers you to respond spontaneously to unexpected situations onstage. You understand your character's core, allowing you to react authentically within the given circumstances, enriching the performance.

Unlocking the Character's Inner World:

- ***Backstory Exploration:*** Dig deeper than the script. Research the character's background, relationships, and past experiences. Understand their hopes, dreams, and vulnerabilities.
- ***Emotional Anchors:*** Identify key moments in the script where your character experiences strong emotions. Connect these moments to personal memories or emotions, allowing you to access authentic feelings onstage.
- ***Sensory Immersion:*** Imagine yourself in your character's shoes. Vividly recreate their sensory experience: sights, sounds, smells, and textures. Allow these details to inform your physicality and emotional responses.

Exercises for Internal Exploration:

- *Character Collage:* Create a collage depicting your character's physical appearance, emotional states, and significant memories. Analyze the collage to gain a deeper understanding of their inner world.
- *Character Journaling:* Write from your character's perspective, expressing their thoughts, feelings, and motivations in response to key events in the script.
- *Character Interview:* Imagine interviewing your character. Ask them questions about their past, relationships, and deepest desires. Listen to their "responses" to gain invaluable insights.

Connecting with the Truth:

- *Method Acting Techniques:* Explore techniques like sensory memory and emotional recall to draw on personal experiences and connect with your character's emotions authentically.
- *Observation and Empathy:* Observe people in everyday life, their mannerisms, emotional expressions, and reactions. Use these observations to enrich your understanding of human behaviour and inform your portrayal.
- *Embrace Vulnerability:* Don't shy away from portraying complex emotions, even pain or vulnerability. Authentic emotional expression resonates with audiences and strengthens their connection to your character.

Beyond the Basics:

- ***Collaboration is Key:*** Discuss your character interpretations with directors, scene partners, and acting coaches. Their perspectives can challenge your assumptions and enrich your understanding.
- ***Stay Open and Fluid:*** Allow your understanding of your character to evolve throughout the rehearsal process. Be open to adapting your portrayal based on new discoveries and insights.
- ***Continuous Exploration:*** Internalization is a lifelong journey, not a one-time destination. Keep honing your skills, exploring new techniques, and seeking inspiration to deepen your connection with characters.

Remember: The path to internalization is unique for every actor. Embrace the journey, experiment with different approaches, and never stop seeking your character's inner truth. When you connect with their soul, your performance transcends mere words and actions, leaving audiences captivated by the raw, emotional power of storytelling.

Bonus Tip: Watch interviews with actors discussing their personal approaches to internalization and finding their characters' truth. Analyze their insights and incorporate them into your own exploration.

---------- **End of Chapter 14** ----------

CHAPTER 15: Conquering the Audition
Mastering Techniques,
Taming Nerves, and Shining Bright

Theory:

The audition room becomes your stage, the casting director your audience, and every second an opportunity to showcase your talent and land your dream role. This chapter equips you with the tools and techniques to navigate the audition process with confidence, overcome the inevitable nerves, and present your best self under pressure.

Understanding the Audition Landscape:

Auditions come in various forms – monologues, scenes, cold readings – each demanding specific preparation and presentation strategies. Knowing the expectations and mastering the basics is crucial for making a lasting impression.

Essential Preparation Techniques:

- *Script Analysis:* Delve into the script, understand the character's motivations, relationships, and emotional journey. Highlight key moments and potential challenges.
- *Rehearse, Refine, Repeat:* Practice your lines thoroughly, paying attention to clarity, pacing, and emotional expression. Experiment with different interpretations and find your unique portrayal.
- *Dress the Part:* Choose attire that reflects the character's personality and the play's setting. Dress professionally while remaining comfortable and confident.

Techniques for Different Formats:

- *Monologues:* Identify the central arc of the monologue, build towards emotional peaks, and vary your vocal dynamics and physicality to captivate the audience.
- *Scenes:* Collaborate with fellow actors, establish natural connections, and react genuinely to their emotions and intentions. Listen actively and respond authentically.
- *Cold Readings:* Sharpen your sight-reading skills and focus on understanding the text quickly. Adapt your characterization based on limited information and make bold choices.

Taming the Audition Jitters:

- ***Practice Mindfulness:*** Engage in breathing exercises and visualization techniques to calm your nerves and centre yourself before the audition.
- ***Positive Affirmations:*** Repeat positive self-talk statements to boost your confidence and remind yourself of your abilities.
- ***Preparation is Power:*** Thorough preparation reduces anxiety. Knowing your material and believing in your choices empowers you to walk into the room with confidence.

Exercises for Audition Success:

- ***Mock Auditions:*** Practice with friends or classmates, simulating real audition scenarios. Receive feedback and refine your presentation based on their observations.
- ***Self-Recording:*** Film yourself performing monologues or scenes. Watch the recordings critically and identify areas for improvement.
- ***Improv Games***: Expand your spontaneity and ability to handle unexpected situations through improv games and exercises.

Beyond the Basics:

- ***Show, Don't Tell:*** Don't simply recite lines; embody the character's emotions and intentions through your physicality, vocal expression, and eye contact.

- ***Make Strong Choices:*** Don't play it safe. Take bold risks, make unique choices, and showcase your individuality and interpretation of the character.
- ***Ask Questions:*** Don't be afraid to ask clarifying questions about the scene or character. Demonstrating initiative and engagement sets you apart.

Remember: Auditions are not mere judgments; they are opportunities to showcase your talent and connect with casting directors. Embrace the process, learn from each experience, and never stop refining your skills. With dedication and preparation, you'll navigate the audition journey with confidence and land roles that ignite your passion for acting.

Bonus Tip: Research casting directors and productions you're interested in. Understanding their preferences and tailoring your approach can increase your chances of success.

---------- **End of Chapter 15** ----------

Conclusion

Congratulations on completing your journey through **"FADE IN"**.

I hope this book has been a valuable resource, providing you with insights, techniques, and inspiration to enhance your skills and deepen your passion for the craft in your acting endeavours.

As you've reached the end of this book, remember that acting is a lifelong journey of growth and discovery. The techniques and exercises you've learnt here is just the beginning. Always remember the magic of storytelling and how you can touch people's hearts by becoming different characters. Whether you're acting on stage, in front of the camera or just for fun; every time you act, you have the chance to make a connection with someone.

I encourage you to continue exploring, practicing, and honing your craft. Seek out opportunities to perform, whether in a school or college production or with your local theatre groups or in short film projects.

Keep practicing, keep learning and keep trying new things. Don't be afraid of the challenges and setbacks—they're all part of the journey. And don't forget to celebrate your successes too!

Let your passion guide you, and let your own unique style shine through in every performance. Most importantly, never forget why you love acting.

Thank you for joining me on this journey through this book. I wish you all the best in your acting adventures ahead.

We will soon meet with the next and final part of this book named **"FADE OUT"**

Best wishes,
Debanshu Shekhar

<u>About the Author</u>

While pursuing his Graduation, **Debanshu Shekhar,** began his theatre journey in 2008 at Maharaja Agrasen College, Delhi University (DU). As an active member of the theatre society 'Abhinay' of his college, Debanshu decided to pursue Theatre as a full-time career.

Following this passion, he applied and got selected on merit to join one of the prestigious Drama Schools of the country: Bhartendu Natya Academy (BNA), Lucknow in 2011 for his post-graduation in Dramatic Arts.

After receiving his Masters in Dramatic Arts degree, he then formed his theatre company 'Naatakwaale' in 2013, which has given more than 1300 shows all over India till date.

He has worked with eminent theatre personalities of the world. He has done 60+ plays all over India. Bhindi, The Loser, Gandh, Home-Maid, The Bait and Stockholm are some of his notable plays under Naatakwaale's production. He has conducted 300+ acting workshops till date under the banner of Naatakwaale by collaborating with different schools, colleges, NGOs and corporate companies. He has trained more than 400 budding actors till 2024.

Currently, he is running his theatre company Naatakwaale, and also working as an actor in different films and TV projects.